ADAM HA

Making Love Last a Lifetime

BIBLICAL PERSPECTIVES ON LOVE, MARRIAGE, AND SEX

LEADER'S GUIDE

BY SALLY D. SHARPE

ABINGDON PRESS
Nashville

Making Love Last a Lifetime:
Biblical Perspectives on Love, Marriage, and Sex

Leader's Guide

Copyright © 2004 by Abingdon Press.

Scripture quotations in this publication, unless otherwise indicated, are from the New Revised Standard Version of the Bible, copyrighted © 1989 by the Division of Christian Education of the National Council of the Churches of Christ in the United States of America, and are used by permission.

Scripture taken from *THE MESSAGE*. Copyright © Eugene H. Peterson, 1993, 1994, 1995. Used by permission of NavPress Publishing Group.

This book is printed on acid-free, elemental chlorine-free paper.

ISBN 0-687-34580-4

04 05 06 07 08 09 10 11 12 13—10 9 8 7 6 5 4 3 2 1
Manufactured in the United States of America.

CONTENTS

How to Use This Leader's Guide

Making Love Last a Lifetime is a video-based small-group study and outreach program that explores love, marriage, and sexuality from a biblical perspective. Its purpose is twofold: to help participants understand God's plan and purpose for love relationships between men and women and the covenant of marriage and to offer real help and hope for achieving the kind of relationship God intends for every couple.

This eight-week program is appropriate for married couples of all ages and stages, as well as for singles who are preparing for marriage or who simply desire to look at scriptural teachings on human sexuality and relationships with the opposite sex. It may be used as a stand-alone study by Sunday school classes and by other small groups meeting at other times during the week. It may also be used as part of a congregational emphasis and outreach event on a topic that holds great interest for singles and married couples both inside and outside the church.

A separate Pastor's Guide with CD-ROM provides all the information and tools needed to take this study beyond the classroom, beyond the sanctuary, and into the community, bringing into the church people who otherwise might attend only at Christmas or Easter. Included in the Pastor's Guide are helpful materials such as suggestions for gathering support and planning worship services; promotional ideas and tools, including materials for a banner, postcard, and poster/flyer; sermon starters, illustrations, and video clips; and more.

Whether you will be leading a stand-alone study or joining other small groups in a congregational emphasis and outreach event, you should emphasize the importance of the participant's book, Adam Hamilton's *Making Love Last a Lifetime: Biblical Perspectives on Love, Marriage, and Sex,* the anchor for the entire program. Encourage group members to use the chapters of the book that correspond to the video presentations in their preparation and follow-up for group sessions. Ideally, participants should have the opportunity to purchase copies of the book prior to your first group session. If this is not possible, introduce them to the book during the first group session and try to obtain copies for them prior to the second session. (Married couples may buy one or two copies, depending on their preference.)

A Quick Overview

As group leader, your role will be to facilitate the weekly sessions using this Leader's Guide and the accompanying video/DVD. Because no two groups are alike, this guide has been designed to give you flexibility and choice in tailoring the sessions for your group. You may choose to follow one of the following format options, *or you may adapt these as you wish to meet the schedule and needs of your particular group.* (Note: The times indicated within parentheses are merely estimates. You may move at a faster or slower pace, making adjustments as necessary to fit your schedule.)

Basic Option: 60 minutes

Opening Prayer . . . . (2 minutes)
Biblical Foundation. . . . . (3 minutes)
Video Presentation . . . . (15 minutes)
Group Discussion . . . . (30 minutes)
Taking It Home . . . . (5 minutes)
Closing Prayer . . . . (< 5 minutes)

Extended Option: 90 minutes

Opening Prayer .... (2 minutes)
Biblical Foundation .... (3 minutes)
Opening Activity .... (10–15 minutes)
Video Presentation .... (15 minutes)
Group Discussion .... (30 minutes)
Group Activity .... (15 minutes)
Taking It Home................................ (5 minutes)
Closing Prayer .... (< 5 minutes)

Although you are encouraged to adapt the sessions to meet your needs, you also are encouraged to make prayer and Scripture *regular* components of the weekly group sessions. Feel free to use the opening and closing prayers provided or to create your own prayers. In either case, the intent is to "cover" the group session in prayer, acknowledging that we are incapable of improving our relationships without God's grace, strength, and help. Likewise, the Scripture verses provided for each session are intended to serve as a biblical foundation for the group session as well as for participants' continuing reflection and application during the following week.

In addition to the components outlined above, the following "leader helps" are provided to equip you for each group session:

Main Idea................................. (session theme)
Session Goals .... (objectives for the group session)
Key Insights .... (summary of main points from the video)
Leader Extra .... (additional information related to the topic)
Notable Quote................ (noteworthy quote from the video)

You may use these helps for your personal preparation only, or you may choose to incorporate them into the group session in some way. For example, you might choose to write the Main Idea and/or Session Goals on a board or chart prior to the beginning of class, review the Key Insights from the video either before or after Group

Discussion, incorporate the Leader Extra into Group Discussion, and close with the Notable Quote.

At the end of the materials provided for each group session, you will find a reproducible handout. (Be sure to photocopy both pages for the group members.) This handout includes an abbreviated summary of the Key Insights from the video and "Taking It Home" application exercises for the coming week. (The exercises can also be found in the participant's book.) Those exercises labeled "Individual Application" are intended for both singles and couples; those labeled "Couple Application" are intended for couples only. Because couples will complete the Individual Application exercises separately, *every* participant will need a copy of the handout. Each week you will have the opportunity to remind participants that these exercises are designed to help them get the most out of this study that they possibly can. They alone are the ones who will determine whether or not this is just another group study or a transformational experience that will have a lasting, positive impact on their lives.

Helpful Hints

Here are a few helpful hints for preparing and leading the weekly group sessions:

- Become familiar with the material before the group session. If possible, watch the video/DVD segment in advance.
- Choose the various components you will use during the group session, including the specific discussion questions you plan to cover. (Highlight these, or put a checkmark beside them.) Remember, you do not have to use all the questions provided; and you even can create your own.
- Secure a TV and video/DVD player in advance; oversee room setup.
- Begin and end on time.
- Be enthusiastic. Remember, you set the tone for the class.
- Create a climate of participation, encouraging individuals to participate as they feel comfortable.
- Communicate the importance of group discussions and group exercises.

- Have couples sit facing each other during group discussion, if possible.
- To stimulate group discussion, consider reviewing the Key Insights first and then asking participants to tell what they saw as the highlights of the video.
- If no one answers at first, do not be afraid of a little silence. Count to seven silently; then say something such as, "Would anyone like to go first?" If no one responds, venture an answer yourself. Then ask for comments and other responses.
- Model openness as you share with the group. Group members will follow your example. If you share at a surface level, everyone else will follow suit.
- Draw out participants without asking them to share what they are unwilling to share. Make eye contact with someone and say something such as, "How about someone else?"
- Encourage multiple answers or responses before moving on.
- Ask "Why?" or "Why do you believe that?" to help continue a discussion and give it greater depth.
- Affirm others' responses with comments such as, "Great" or "Thanks" or "Good insight"—especially if this is the first time someone has spoken during the group session.
- Give everyone a chance to talk, but keep the conversation moving. Moderate to prevent a few individuals from doing all the talking.
- Monitor your own contributions. If you are doing most of the talking, back off so that you do not train the group not to respond.
- Remember that you do not have to have all the answers. Your job is to keep the discussion going and encourage participation.
- Honor the time schedule. If a session is running longer than expected, get consensus from the group before continuing beyond the agreed-upon ending time.
- Consider involving group members in various aspects of the group session, such as asking for volunteers to run the video/DVD, read the prayers or say their own, read the Scripture, and so forth.

Above all, remember to pray. Pray for God to prepare and guide you, pray for your group members by name and for whatever God may do in their hearts and lives, and pray for God's presence and guidance before each group session. Prayer will both encourage and empower you for the weeks ahead.

Finally, if you are a first-time leader, remember that many characters in the Bible were hesitant and unsure of accepting God's call to lead; but God never abandoned any of them. Rest assured that God will be with you, too. After all, Jesus promised, "I am with you always, to the end of the age" (Matthew 28:20).

Venus and Mars in the Beginning

Main Idea: Love, marriage, and sex are God's idea.

Getting Started

Session Goals

This session is intended to help participants ...

- better understand God's plan and purpose for love, marriage, and sex;
- remember the importance of inviting God to take control of our relationships, allowing the Holy Spirit to work through us;
- have hope that—with God's help—they may experience the level of joy, love, and happiness God intends for every marriage;
- understand how to make the most of the study through personal application (using the reproducible handout and the accompanying participant's book).

Opening Prayer

Dear God, we acknowledge that you created love, marriage, and sex; they were *your* idea. Open our hearts, and give us godly wisdom so that we may better understand your plan and purpose for these beautiful gifts you have given us. Meet us where we are (whether single or married), guiding and directing us according to your calling on our lives. We know there are damaged relationships that need your healing; and we pray that, beginning today and continuing throughout this study, you will tear down walls and provide real help and hope. Give us the perspectives and skills that will allow our relationships to soar to heights we never imagined possible; and, if our relationships are already strong, help us to grow even more in our capacity to love so that we may experience all the fullness you have in store for us. In Jesus' name we pray. Amen.

Biblical Foundation

Then the LORD God said, "It is not good that the man should be alone; I will make him a helper as his partner."... So the LORD God caused a deep sleep to fall upon the man, and he slept; then he took one of his ribs and closed up its place with flesh. And the rib that the LORD God had taken from the man he made into a woman and brought her to the man. Then the man said,

> *"This at last is bone of my bones*
> *and flesh of my flesh;*
> *this one shall be called Woman,*
> *for out of Man this one was taken."*

Therefore a man leaves his father and his mother and clings to his wife, and they become one flesh. And the man and his wife were both naked, and were not ashamed. (Genesis 2:18, 21-25)

Opening Activity

Create a "Top 10" list of things that make a marriage strong. Have participants call out ideas as you write them on a board or chart. Do not take time to discuss or debate the ideas or their level of importance. Simply list and number them as they are named. Tell the group that you will keep the list and refer back to it in your last session together (Week 8).

Learning Together

Video Presentation

Play the video/DVD segment for Week 1, *Venus and Mars in the Beginning.*
Running Time 15:32

Key Insights

1. God created men and women to be different. These differences are a gift, not a curse; they are to be valued and understood, not hated and despised. Our differences are essential to God's plan.
2. Men and women need each other. We are not complete by ourselves. This does not mean that *everyone* should be married. According to the New Testament, it is a high calling of God to remain single so that one is free to devote one's whole life and time to service for Christ (1 Corinthians 7). Still, whether single or married, we need companions of the opposite sex who see the world through a different set of eyes and bless us with their uniqueness and gifts.
3. Sex and sexuality were meant to be beautiful; God designed them as a good part of creation. (Note: The reference in Genesis 2:24 to clinging to each other and becoming one flesh is a euphemism for sexual intercourse.)
4. The union of a man and woman (marriage) was designed by God as the solution to a problem. The problem was that the first human was alone and needed companionship; he was unable to live as God intended without a partner. God designed marriage as a way of meeting the basic needs of human beings for companionship and help (Genesis 2:20-25).
5. Marriage is a sacred calling from God to serve, give to, and sacrifice for another. Choosing to marry is choosing to answer this calling toward the person you are marrying, although you may not always *feel* like it. In fact, you cannot answer the calling unless you allow the power of the Holy Spirit to work through you, helping you to rise above your self-centeredness. To the degree that you focus on this calling, you will find joy and meaning in your marriage, even when things are not perfect.

Leader Extra

The Bible has much to say about love, marriage, and sex.
• One of the first stories in the Bible is about marriage and the relationship between a man and a woman (Genesis 2).

- Throughout the Law of Moses (the first five books of the Old Testament), issues of marriage and sexuality come up again and again.
- An entire book of the Bible, the Song of Solomon (also known as the Song of Songs), is devoted to romantic love.
- The prophets and the writers of Proverbs address the topics of love, marriage, and sex on numerous occasions (for example, Ezra 9:12-14; Nehemiah 13:25; Proverbs 5:18-19; Jeremiah 29:6; Malachi 2:13-15).
- Jesus performs his first miracle at a wedding (John 2:1-12), likens himself to a bridegroom (Matthew 9:15), uses a wedding as the setting of a parable (Matthew 25:1-13), and offers a wide variety of teachings that are directly applicable to marriage.
- The apostle Paul calls marriage a "mystery" that portrays the love of Christ for the church (Ephesians 5:31-32). Paul frequently addresses issues of how men and women are meant to relate together, including matters of the marriage bed (1 Corinthians 7; Ephesians 5:21-33).
- Throughout Scripture, God's relationship with us—first with Israel and, later, also with the church—is likened to a husband's relationship with his bride (Isaiah 54:5; Ezekiel 16:8; Hosea 2:14-20; John 3:28-30; Revelation 19:7-8).

Group Discussion

1. What evidence do we have that love, marriage, and sex are important to God? (If time allows, read and discuss several passages of Scripture from the Leader Extra.)
2. Why is it important to invite God to be a part of the marriage relationship? What does this mean and involve? What happens when God is left out of the marriage relationship?
3. In what ways does our "human condition" complicate our relationships? Give a few examples to illustrate.
4. What does the Creation story in Genesis 2 tell us about God's purpose and plan for marriage? (See verses 18, 21-25.)
5. Name and briefly discuss some of the differences between men and women (other than physical differences). What can we do to help keep these differences from causing conflict in our relationships with the opposite sex?

6. Apart from procreation, why do men and women truly *need* each other? Even if someone has no desire to marry, why is it important for that person to have friends of the opposite sex? Tell how your spouse "complements" or "balances" you. If single, how have friendships with the opposite sex enriched your life?
7. In what ways does our culture promote the idea that sex is dirty, vulgar, or cheap? What can we do within our families, the church, and the community to "reclaim" and affirm the sacredness and beauty of God's gift of sex for husband and wife?
8. What does it mean to say that marriage is a sacred calling from God? How should this understanding affect your relationship with your spouse—or, if single, your attitude toward marriage?
9. How has this discussion helped or challenged you?

Group Activity
Divide participants into two or more groups. Have each group write a "classified" ad written by God for the calling of marriage. The ad should spell out some of the basic requirements necessary for fulfilling God's calling to minister to another person in marriage. Tell the groups that they may include appropriate Bible passages if they choose. When you come back together, briefly compare and discuss the ads.

Wrapping Up

Taking It Home
Explain that there are two resources available to help participants with personal application each week.

First, there is the Participant Handout. Briefly review the Taking It Home application exercises included in the handout. Explain that Individual Application exercises are intended for both singles and couples, and Couple Application exercises are intended for couples only. Couples will want to complete the Individual Application exercises separately and the Couple Application exercises together. Encourage participants to complete the activities during the coming week, and reassure them that they will not be asked to share any details with the group. The exercises are intended for their private use and are designed to help them get the most out of this study that they possibly can. They alone are the ones who will determine whether or not this is just another group study or a transformational experience that will have a lasting, positive impact on their lives.

Second, there is the accompanying participant's book, *Making Love Last a Lifetime,* by Adam Hamilton, which expands on the material covered in the weekly video presentations. Invite those participants who have already purchased copies of the book to read the first chapter this week as a follow-up to this group session. (Note: Acknowledge that some participants may choose to read the corresponding chapters in *advance* of the group sessions week to week, which also is acceptable. It is a matter of preference.) Those participants who have not ordered or purchased copies of the book may want to do so now.

Notable Quote
"You might have a great marriage, but until you've invited God to be a part, ... until you've understood God's plan for marriage, you have settled for less, not the best."
—*Adam Hamilton*

Closing Prayer
Lord God, thank you for this time of learning and sharing. We are so grateful for the loving care you show us through all the loving relationships in our lives—especially our marriages. Help us to consider the insights we have gained today and use them to improve both our attitudes and our relationships. As we continue our study in the weeks ahead, enable us to understand more fully your plan and purposes for marriage. May we draw closer to each other as we draw closer to you. In Jesus' name we pray. Amen.

Week 1: Venus and Mars in the Beginning
Participant Handout

Then the LORD God said, "It is not good that the man should be alone;
I will make him a helper as his partner."... So the LORD God caused
a deep sleep to fall upon the man, and he slept; then he took one of his
ribs and closed up its place with flesh. And the rib that the LORD God
had taken from the man he made into a woman and brought her to the
man. Then the man said,
"This at last is bone of my bones
and flesh of my flesh;
this one shall be called Woman,
for out of Man this one was taken."
Therefore a man leaves his father and his mother and clings to his wife,
and they become one flesh. And the man and his wife were both naked,
and were not ashamed. (Genesis 2:18, 21-25)

Key Insights

1. God created men and women to be different; these differences are a gift, not a curse. They are to be valued and understood, not hated and despised. Our differences are essential to God's plan.
2. Men and women need each other. We are not complete by ourselves. Whether single or married, we need companions of the opposite sex.
3. Sex and sexuality were meant to be beautiful; they were designed by God as a good part of creation.
4. The union of a man and woman (marriage) was designed by God as a way of meeting the basic needs of two human beings for companionship and help.
5. Marriage is a sacred calling from God to give, serve, and sacrifice for another. We cannot answer this calling unless we allow the power of the Holy Spirit to work through us, helping us to rise above self-centeredness. To the degree that we focus on this calling, we will find joy and meaning in marriage, even when things are not perfect.

Taking It Home

Individual Application
- Read one-to-two chapters of the Song of Solomon each day this week, asking yourself the following questions: What are the various characters feeling in this chapter? What do they do that fosters their love? How can we learn from their example?
- Find one or more ways to affirm and celebrate the differences of your spouse—or, if single, someone special of the opposite sex— (for example, do something he or she likes to do; look for the positive side of something you ordinarily consider negative or irritating; offer genuine praise for one of his or her differences; and so forth).
- List all the reasons you need and appreciate your spouse—or, if single, someone special of the opposite sex. Give thanks to God for these gifts *each day this week.*

Couple Application
- Talk together about those irritations that can build up, leading to resentment and conflict. Agree up front to speak the truth in love and listen to each other without debating or becoming defensive. Commit to pray about these things throughout the week, asking God to change your hearts and attitudes. End by sharing the lists you compiled of the reasons you need and appreciate each other.

What Women Wish Men Knew About Women

Main Idea: A woman's heart is like a love bank.

Getting Started

Session Goals
This session is intended to help participants ...
- understand how a woman's heart is like a love bank, requiring more deposits than withdrawals;
- identify a woman's needs and ways to fill up her love bank;
- recognize the importance of having a partnership in faith.

Opening Prayer
Dear God, as we come here today, seeking your wisdom and guidance for our relationships, we ask you to soften our hearts and remove any resentment or pride that might cause us to be accusatory or defensive. May this not be a "gripe session," Lord, but an opportunity to understand each other better as we allow the Holy Spirit to guide our tongues and open our ears. We thank you in advance for the insights you will give us today about women and their needs. In Jesus' name we pray. Amen.

Biblical Foundation
Husbands, love your wives, just as Christ loved the church and gave himself up for her. (Ephesians 5:25)

19

As God's chosen ones, holy and beloved, clothe yourselves with compassion, kindness, humility, meekness, and patience. Bear with one another and, if anyone has a complaint against another, forgive each other; just as the Lord has forgiven you, so you also must forgive. Above all, clothe yourselves with love, which binds everything together in perfect harmony. And let the peace of Christ rule in your hearts, to which indeed you were called in the one body. And be thankful. Let the word of Christ dwell in you richly; teach and admonish one another in all wisdom; and with gratitude in your hearts sing psalms, hymns, and spiritual songs to God. And whatever you do, in word or deed, do everything in the name of the Lord Jesus, giving thanks to God the Father through him. (Colossians 3:12-17)

Opening Activity

Separate the men and women into two groups, and have each group write a response to the following question: What makes a woman feel loved? Have them put a check beside anything that relates specifically to wives and husbands only. When you come back together, have one person from each group share the group's responses. (If possible, provide chart paper for each group to write on so that you may post the responses for the duration of the session.)

Learning Together

Video Presentation

Play the video/DVD segment for Week 2, *What Women Wish Men Knew About Women.*
Running Time 14:46

Key Insights

1. Men and women have different needs. This is part of God's plan, so that we complement and complete each other. Because of these differences, it takes some adjustments, a willingness to listen, and just plain work for both individuals to be content and even joyful in their relationship.

2. A woman's heart is like a "love bank." Actions on the part of both the man and the woman constitute deposits and withdrawals from the woman's love bank. Women can operate with a deficit account for long periods of time. The overdraft warnings a woman gives may take the form of a short temper or irritation, coldness to physical advances, or tears. Sometimes when she tries to say that she is overdrawn, the man becomes defensive or angry and does not hear what she is saying—and she becomes even more overdrawn. When a woman's love bank operates in overdraft mode for a long period of time, it eventually goes bankrupt and the account becomes closed. She has nothing left to give. In marriage, many times this status is formalized when she expresses her desire for a divorce.

3. Women feel loved when men ...
   • demonstrate affection through nonsexual touch, words, and small acts of kindness;
   • pay attention to them by listening, valuing their thoughts, noticing what is important to them, inviting them to share their feelings, and sharing their own innermost thoughts;
   • are genuinely engaged in the home and family, loving the children and helping with household duties;
   • express appreciation and gratitude for who they are and what they have done, rather than taking them for granted or criticizing them;
   • are partners in faith with them (praying together, worshiping together, growing spiritually together).

Leader Extra

Philippians 2:1-18 is an excellent summary of what it means to embody the love of Christ. Consider encouraging participants to use the following prayer, based on this passage, for the remainder of the study. Couples might want to replace the underlined words with each other's name.

Lord, today help me to
• have the mind of Christ;
• embody the love of Christ;

- do nothing from selfish ambition or conceit;
- be humble, putting <u>others</u> before myself;
- care more about the needs and interests of <u>others</u> than I do about my own;
- serve <u>others</u> in obedience to God, modeling the example of Christ;
- do all things without grumbling or arguing;
- and remember that I cannot do any of these things without you living and working in me.

Amen.

Group Discussion

1. Why do you think men often do not understand the needs of women? Do you think women are any better at understanding men? Why or why not?
2. What is the most important thing you have learned about the opposite sex? When and how did you learn this? Share something you have learned about the opposite sex "the hard way."
3. Does the metaphor of a woman's heart being like a love bank ring true with your own experience? If not, why? If so, give an example to illustrate.
4. Share a time when you were not paying enough attention to the love of your life—whether or not you realized it at the time. What was the reason behind your inattentiveness?
5. List and discuss things that make a woman feel closer to the man in her life. (Note: You might want to skip this question if you will be doing the following group activity.)
6. Why is it important to be able to "open up" to the woman or man you love? Give an example from your own experience.
7. How is listening an act of love? What traits make someone a good listener? How can real listening reduce conflict in a relationship? (See James 1:19.)
8. How is a relationship enriched when a man is in touch with his spiritual life? How would you define what it means to be "partners in faith"?
9. Discuss today's Biblical Foundations (Ephesians 5:25 and Colossians 3:12-17). What does it mean to "clothe yourselves

with love"? What does it mean to love someone as Christ loved the church? Why do you think husbands, specifically, are called to do this?
10. How has this discussion helped or challenged you?

Group Activity
Brainstorm some creative ways to make deposits into a woman's love bank. Have fun with this! (The men in the group might want to take notes!)

Wrapping Up

Taking It Home
Briefly review the Taking It Home application exercises included in the Participant Handout. Remind participants that Individual Application exercises are intended for both singles and couples, and Couple Application exercises are intended for couples only. Couples will want to complete the Individual Application exercises separately and the Couple Application exercises together.

Encourage participants to complete the activities during the coming week, reminding them that they will not be asked to share any details with the group. The exercises are intended for their private use and are designed to help them get the most out of this study that they possibly can. (Note: This week the men have more exercises than the women. Reassure participants that next week the tables will be turned!)

Invite those who have purchased copies of the participant's book to read Chapter 2 this week as a follow-up to this group session. (Those reading chapters in advance of the group sessions will read Chapter 3 this week.)

Notable Quote
"[Men,] you are called to be the physical presentation of Jesus to [the woman you love]. You are not called to always be madly in love with her. You are not called to always be overwhelmed with feelings.... You have been called to understand that this woman has needs that God

created you to meet—and then to sacrifice yourself in order to minister to those needs."

—Adam Hamilton

Closing Prayer
O God, you know that in this very room there are women—as well as men—whose love banks are empty. Some of them have been overdrawn for some time. In fact, there may be some who are considering filing for "bankruptcy." Fill these hearts with your love right now so that they might, through your strength, find the grace and the ability to love again. Where there is brokenness, bring healing. Forgive us all for the ways that we take and take without giving back. Forgive us for failing to treasure the loves of our lives as your greatest gifts to us after Christ. Teach us to love following his example. In his name we pray. Amen.

Week 2: What Women Wish Men Knew About Women
Participant Handout

Husbands, love your wives, just as Christ loved the church and gave himself up for her. (Ephesians 5:25)

As God's chosen ones, holy and beloved, clothe yourselves with compassion, kindness, humility, meekness, and patience. Bear with one another and, if anyone has a complaint against another, forgive each other; just as the Lord has forgiven you, so you also must forgive. Above all, clothe yourselves with love, which binds everything together in perfect harmony. And let the peace of Christ rule in your hearts, to which indeed you were called in the one body. And be thankful. Let the word of Christ dwell in you richly; teach and admonish one another in all wisdom; and with gratitude in your hearts sing psalms, hymns, and spiritual songs to God. And whatever you do, in word or deed, do everything in the name of the Lord Jesus, giving thanks to God the Father through him. (Colossians 3:12-17)

Key Insights
1. Because men and women have different needs, it takes some adjustments, a willingness to listen, and just plain work for both individuals to be content and even joyful in their relationship.
2. A woman's heart is like a "love bank." Actions on the part of both the man and the woman constitute deposits and withdrawals. The overdraft warnings a woman gives may take the form of a short temper or irritation, coldness to physical advances, or tears. When a woman's love bank operates in overdraft mode for a long period of time, it eventually goes bankrupt; she has nothing left to give.
3. Women feel loved when men ...
   * demonstrate affection through nonsexual touch, words, and small acts of kindness;
   * pay attention to them by listening, valuing their thoughts, noticing what is important to them, inviting them to share their feelings, and sharing their own innermost thoughts;
   * are genuinely engaged in the home and family, loving the children and helping with household duties;

- express appreciation and gratitude for who they are and what they have done, rather than taking them for granted or criticizing them;
- are partners in faith with them.

Taking It Home

Individual Application
- Look over the list of what makes women feel loved in Key Insight #3. Women: Which of these are you most in need of? Men: Which of these do you need to work on?
- Men only: Read 1 Corinthians 13:1-8a. Insert your name in the place of "love" and "it" in verses 4-7 to see how you measure up to God's desires.
- Men only: In Proverbs 31:10-31, we see a husband expressing gratitude for his wife. Pray a prayer of thanksgiving for the woman you love. Then write a Proverbs 31 letter for her—a poem or note thanking her for all she has done for you. Praise, affirm, and encourage her. Give it to her on your date (See the second bulleted point under Couple Application.).
- Husbands only: Read Ephesians 5:25. What are the practical implications of this verse for your marriage?

Couple Application
- Discuss your responses to the first bulleted point under Individual Application. Men: Ask, "What can I do for you to bless and encourage you? When do you feel closest to me? Are there things I do that push you away?"
- Men: Plan a date for this week. If a traditional night out is not possible, consider having a lunch date or a late-night "at-home" date. Remember to share your letter.

What Men Wish Women Knew About Men

Main Idea: Men have a deep need to be admired and affirmed.

Getting Started

Session Goals
This session is intended to help participants...
- understand that a man's heart is also like a love bank;
- identify a man's needs and ways to fill up his love bank;
- discuss the importance of affirming and respecting a man;
- understand what it means to "be subject to one another out of reverence for Christ."

Opening Prayer
Dear God, once again we come seeking your wisdom and guidance for our relationships; and, once again, we ask you to soften our hearts and remove any resentment or pride that might cause us to be either accusatory or defensive. May this not be a "gripe session," Lord, but an opportunity to understand each other better as we allow the Holy Spirit to guide our tongues and open our ears. We thank you in advance for the insights you will give us today about men and their needs. In Jesus' name we pray. Amen.

Biblical Foundation
Be subject to one another out of reverence for Christ.
Wives, be subject to your husbands as you are to the Lord. For the hus-

band is the head of the wife just as Christ is the head of the church, the body of which he is the Savior. Just as the church is subject to Christ, so also wives ought to be, in everything, to their husbands. . . .

Each of you [husbands], however, should love his wife as himself, and a wife should respect her husband. (Ephesians 5:21-24, 33)

Leader Extra

For generations, this passage from Ephesians has been misused and abused, leading in some cases to the oppression of women. During the past thirty years there has been an understandable backlash, in which some women have condemned this passage of Scripture and even suggested excising it from the Bible. Once we get past the misconceptions and misinterpretations, however, this passage contains some important truths. It may be helpful for your group to read the passage in several versions, including a contemporary version. Read these versions for the Biblical Foundation, and delve into the meanings of the passage during Group Discussion. Here are some points to consider as part of that discussion:

- Dr. Elizabeth Achtemeir, Professor of Bible at Union Theological Seminary, writes of the passage:

  This does not mean that wives are to worship their husbands, to obey them unquestioningly, or to elevate them to the place of God. . . . Rather, wives are to act toward their husbands as the church should act toward Christ—in faithfulness, in love, in service, in honor, in devotion—because what the wife does to her husband she is in fact doing to Christ."[1]

- In this context, to "be subject to"—or to "submit," as it is sometimes stated—essentially means to "be courteously reverent" (Ephesians 5:21 in *The Message*). For wives, this means understanding and supporting their husbands. For husbands, this means cherishing and loving their wives as Christ cherished and loved the church.
- In order to be honored and to be deserving of a wife who reverences him, a man must be worthy of her respect by loving her as

28

Christ loved the church. A marriage based on the Bible requires both sides of the equation: a husband who loves as Christ does and seeks to meet the needs of his wife and a wife who honors as the church does and seeks to meet the needs of her husband.

Opening Activity

Separate the men and women into two groups; then have each group write a response to the following question: What makes a man feel loved? Have them put a check beside anything that relates specifically to wives and husbands only. When you come back together, have one person from each group share the group's responses. (If possible, provide chart paper for each group to write on so that you may post the responses for the duration of the session.)

Learning Together

Video Presentation

Play the video/DVD segment for Week 3, *What Men Wish Women Knew About Men.*
Running Time 14:29

Key Insights

1. A man's heart is also like a love bank, with one exception: The currency needed to fill up his love bank is *different* than that needed by a woman.
2. God designed the male psyche to include a need to provide for, care for, and impress the woman he loves. Most men want to be her hero, so that she will admire and be proud of him. So, the primary way a man feels loved is when the woman he loves expresses genuine admiration and affirmation.
3. Other ways a man feels loved are when ...
   • she listens to him and encourages him to share important things (Note: The key here is talking about what is important to *him.*);
   • she cares for his physical and emotional needs (and those of the children, if any) through acts of service (Note: Men often take women for granted in this area, failing to express and demon-

strate their appreciation. While such acts of service are deposits into a man's love bank, they are actually withdrawals from a woman's love bank. Words of appreciation for her acts of service will help to replenish her love bank.);
- she (his wife) is sexually intimate with him;
- she spends quality time with him, especially doing things together (recreational companionship).

4. A man needs his "down time." John Gray refers to this as "cave time," which is time alone to process his thoughts.
5. A man does not like being expected to read a woman's mind. He appreciates her telling him what she is thinking or what she needs or wants.
6. A man needs to be needed—without the woman he loves being *overly* needy—and to know that he makes a difference in her life. He wants to be her "knight in shining armor."

Group Discussion
1. Why do you think admiration is high on the list for men? Why do you think God designed the male psyche to include this need? Do you think most women realize that a man's primary need is for the woman he loves to be proud of him? Why or why not?
2. Discuss the power of an act of praise. Share a time when you experienced this power as either a giver or a receiver.
3. Both women and men have a need to talk and share with the opposite sex. How is a man's need different from a woman's?
4. How does a man's need for "acts of service" sometimes create a vicious cycle of withdrawals from both her and his love bank? What can men and women do to help each other in this area? (See the related comment included in Key Insights.)
5. Do you agree with the survey results that suggest sexual fulfillment is a higher priority to a man at some times in his life and less important at other times? Why or why not?
6. Discuss the similarities and differences in the kind of "quality time" men and women desire to spend with each other. Share some tips for spending more quality time together.
7. List and discuss the three not-so-secret "secrets" about men. (See Key Insights 4–6).

8. Discuss today's Biblical Foundation (Ephesians 5:21-24, 33) and what it means in the context of a healthy Christian marriage. What does it mean for a woman to "be subject to" or "submit" to her husband? What is the husband's responsibility? What kind of "leadership" is he to provide? (See the discussion points included in the Leader Extra on pages 28–29.)
9. How has this discussion helped or challenged you?

Leader Extra
Single men and women in the group may find this information particularly interesting. One hundred fifty single men of all ages* responded to the questions, "What do you find most appealing or attractive in a woman?" and "What makes a woman unattractive?" Here are their responses:

Attractive	Unattractive
1. Christian faith	1. Insecure/needy/low self-esteem
2. Attractive looks	2. Conceited
3. Sense of humor	3. Not caring for body/hygiene/appearance
4. Intelligence	4. Smoking
5. Similar interests	5. Disrespectful
6. Strong morals	6. Bad/negative attitude
	7. Lying

* In a survey conducted at the United Methodist Church of the Resurrection

Group Activity
Brainstorm some creative ways to make deposits into a man's love bank. Have fun with this! (The women in the group might want to take notes!)

Wrapping Up

Taking It Home
Briefly review the Taking It Home application exercises included in the Participant Handout. Encourage participants to complete the activities during the coming week, reminding them that they will not be asked to share any details with the group. The exercises are intended for their private use and are designed to help them get the most out of this study that they possibly can. (Note: This week the women have more exercises than the men.)

Invite those who have purchased copies of the participant's book to read Chapter 3 this week as a follow-up to this group session. (Those reading chapters in advance of the group sessions will read Chapter 4 this week.)

Notable Quote
"[Women,] don't think your husband, by himself, is going to become the man of your dreams. You're setting yourself up for a disappointment. But you can help make him, not the man of your dreams, but the man God dreams him to be. This is a powerful thing.... [Your] power is in [your] praise."

—Adam Hamilton

Closing Prayer
Loving God, there are men and women here today who are struggling in their relationships. Help every man here today to be a man of integrity, a man worthy of admiration and respect and honor. Help the men to love, sacrificially, the women in their lives. And help the women to shape their men with their praise and encouragement and blessings. Increase our love, O God, and help us mirror your love in Jesus. In his name we pray. Amen.

---

[1] From *The Committed Marriage,* by Elizabeth Achtemeir (Westminster Press, 1976); page 85.

Week 3: What Men Wish Women Knew About Men
Participant Handout

Be subject to one another out of reverence for Christ.
Wives, be subject to your husbands as you are to the Lord. For the husband is the head of the wife just as Christ is the head of the church, the body of which he is the Savior. Just as the church is subject to Christ, so also wives ought to be, in everything, to their husbands....
Each of you [husbands], however, should love his wife as himself, and a wife should respect her husband. *(Ephesians 5:21-24, 33)*

Key Insights

1. A man's heart is also like a love bank, but the currency needed to fill up his love bank is *different* than that needed by a woman.
2. The primary way a man feels loved is when the woman he loves expresses genuine admiration and affirmation.
3. Other ways a man feels loved are when...
   - she listens to him and encourages him to share important things (Note: The key is talking about what is important to *him*.);
   - she cares for his physical and emotional needs (and those of the children, if any) through acts of service (Note: While such acts of service are deposits into his love bank, they are withdrawals from her love bank. Words of appreciation will help to replenish her love bank.);
   - she (his wife) is sexually intimate with him;
   - she spends quality time with him, especially doing things together (recreational companionship).
4. A man needs his "down time."
5. A man does not like being expected to read a woman's mind. He appreciates her telling him what she is thinking or what she needs or wants.
6. A man needs to be needed (without the woman he loves being *overly* needy).

Taking It Home

Individual Application
- Look over the list of what makes men feel loved in Key Insights 2–3. Men: Which of these are you most in need of? Women: Which of these do you need to work on?
- Women only: Read 1 Corinthians 13:1-8a. Insert your name in the place of "love" and "it" in verses 4-7 to see how you measure up to God's desires.
- Women only: List all the things about the man you love that are unique, special, or praiseworthy. What about his character is good? What does he do that makes a difference? Write him a note of encouragement and thanks. Leave it for him to read when he has some time alone.
- Wives only: Read Ephesians 5:21-24, 33. How can you communicate respect and honor to your husband?

Couple Application
- Sit down together and discuss your responses to the first bulleted point under Individual Application. Women: Ask, "What can I do for you to bless and encourage you? When do you feel closest to me? Are there things I do that push you away?"
- Women: Plan to do something as a couple this week that he enjoys doing.

After the Honeymoon Is Over

Main Idea: Lasting love requires a commitment to do love even when you do not feel love.

Getting Started

Session Goals

This session is intended to help participants ...

- discuss what happens to a marriage when confronted by the everyday pressures of life and the joyful but stressful pressures of starting a family;
- consider strategies for rekindling love in a relationship;
- explore biblical principles that can strengthen love and make it last.

Opening Prayer

Dear God, there are many ups and downs on the rocky road of love. The stress and strain of daily life and the monotony of mundane routines can rob us of our feelings, leaving us empty and dry. Yet we acknowledge that you are our hope. You are the one who revives our hearts of stone and gives us hearts of flesh again. You are the one who gives us the capacity to begin anew. You are the one who brings revival in our relationships—with you and with each other. So, today we pray that you will renew the hearts and lives and relationships of those who are in a hard place and give all of us encouragement, hope, and practical help for growing through the inevitable bumps and dips yet to come. Lord, fill us with your Holy Spirit; and teach us how to clothe ourselves with love—even when we do not feel like it. In Jesus' name we pray. Amen.

Biblical Foundation

As God's chosen ones, holy and beloved, clothe yourselves with compassion, kindness, humility, meekness, and patience. Bear with one another and, if anyone has a complaint against another, forgive each other; just as the Lord has forgiven you, so you also must forgive. Above all, clothe yourselves with love, which binds everything together in perfect harmony.

(Colossians 3:12-14)

Opening Activity

Ask participants to respond to this question: What makes a marriage (or dating relationship) vibrant and "alive"? List the responses on a board or chart for all to see.

Learning Together

Video Presentation

Play the video/DVD segment for Week 4, *After the Honeymoon Is Over.*

Running Time 15:07

Key Insights

1. The key to a lasting relationship—and to reviving or "divorce-proofing" a marriage—is not in how you resolve conflict or disagreements but in "how you are with each other when you're not fighting."[1] For a relationship or marriage to be successful, there must be more positive than negative feelings, words, and experiences. (Gottman suggests that the magic ratio is five to one—five positive affirmations for every conflict.)

2. A couple's relationship thrives when they *cultivate a friendship* by ...
   - learning about each other (getting to know each other's likes and dislikes, interests, thoughts, and friends);
   - nurturing their fondness and admiration for each other;
   - turning toward each other (spending time together, paying attention to each other, and connecting verbally);
   - allowing themselves to be influenced by each other (for example, shared decision making).
3. Colossians 3:12-14 offers a recipe for a successful friendship, a deep partnership, and a blessed love relationship; but we can follow this advice only if we invite God to help. On our own, we cannot reach our potential for patience, compassion, or forgiveness.
4. We do not always *feel* love. Lasting love requires something much deeper than feelings; it requires a commitment to following Christ in serving another human being. It begins and ends with friendship and a commitment to "do love" even when we do not feel it.

Leader Extra

What does it mean to *do* love even when we do not *feel* love? According to Colossians 3:12-14, it means choosing to ...
- be compassionate and kind (ask ourselves, "What would Jesus do?");
- be humble (think more of others' needs and interests than of our own);
- be gentle and considerate (use words that build up, not tear down);
- be patient (overlook others' flaws and irritating habits);
- forgive (remember how much we have been forgiven);
- love others as ourselves (treat others the way we want to be treated);
- be a peacemaker, not an agitator (settle differences peaceably, without creating or fueling conflict).

For those of us who are in Christ, this is the way we are to treat others—especially the one woman or man God has specifically entrusted to our care. Doing these things makes for a great friendship and a great marriage, but ...

How is it possible? Well, we cannot do it alone. On our own, we cannot reach our potential for patience, compassion, or forgiveness. We can do so *only* if we invite God to help us. When we are connected to Christ through God's Word and prayer and allow the Holy Spirit to work in us, these virtues become not only a possibility but also a reality. In Christ, we have everything we need to *do* love even when we do not *feel* love.

Group Discussion

1. Briefly share how you felt the first few months after your marriage. What were the toughest and easiest adjustments? Or, if you are in a dating relationship (or have been in one in the past), how did the relationship change after the "newness" wore off?
2. Talk about how the first baby changes a marriage. Consider the impact a baby makes on the mother, on the father, and on both parents. How can a husband and wife nurture their relationship during this difficult adjustment period?
3. When a couple has a fight, what impact does it have on the relationship? Discuss both the good and bad aspects of verbal disagreements.
4. List some ways you can cultivate a friendship with the man or woman you love. Give some examples from your own experience.
5. Discuss the importance and rationale of allowing your partner to influence you. Practically speaking, what does this mean?
6. List and discuss some common reasons that couples "fall out of love."
7. What should a couple do when the feelings are gone? Read today's Biblical Foundation, Colossians 3:12-14. Brainstorm some practical ways a couple can live out these verses even when they do not feel like it. Do you believe these actions will help the feelings to return again? Why or why not? Share from your own experience as possible.
8. How has this discussion helped or challenged you?

Group Activity

Ask participants to name things they enjoyed or appreciated in the early days of their relationship. Now compare this list to the list you created at the beginning of class. Are there any duplications or similarities? Encourage participants to begin doing some of these things again this week!

Wrapping Up

Taking It Home
Briefly review the Taking It Home application exercises included in the Participant Handout. Encourage participants to complete the activities during the coming week, reminding them that they will not be asked to share any details with the group. The exercises are intended for their private use and are designed to help them get the most out of this study that they possibly can.

Invite those who have purchased copies of the participant's book to read Chapter 4 this week as a follow-up to this group session. (Those reading chapters in advance of the group sessions will read Chapter 5 this week.)

Notable Quote
"Mature love is doing love, even when you don't feel it. When you persistently do loving things towards another person, an amazing thing happens: The doing produces the feelings."

—*Adam Hamilton*

Closing Prayer
Lord God, thank you for the help and hope you have offered us today. As we prepare to leave this place, we ask you once again to fill us with your Holy Spirit and make us into the men and women you long for us to be. Be our sole sufficiency, Lord, helping us to *do* love until we *feel* it. In Jesus' name we pray. Amen.

---

[1]From *Why Marriages Succeed or Fail*, by John Gottman (Fireside, 1995); page 46.

Week 4: After the Honeymoon Is Over
Participant Handout

As God's chosen ones, holy and beloved, clothe yourselves with compassion, kindness, humility, meekness, and patience. Bear with one another and, if anyone has a complaint against another, forgive each other; just as the Lord has forgiven you, so you also must forgive. Above all, clothe yourselves with love, which binds everything together in perfect harmony. (Colossians 3:12-14)

Key Insights

1. For a relationship or marriage to be successful, there must be more positive than negative feelings, words, and experiences. (Author John Gottman suggests a ratio of five positive affirmations for every conflict.)
2. A couple's relationship thrives when they *cultivate a friendship* by ...
   - learning about each other;
   - nurturing their fondness and admiration for each other;
   - turning toward each other (spending time together, connecting verbally);
   - allowing themselves to be influenced by each other (for example, shared decision making).
3. Colossians 3:12-14 offers a recipe for strong relationships, but we can follow this advice only if we are connected to Christ and allow the Holy Spirit to work in us.
4. We do not always *feel* love. Lasting love begins and ends with friendship and a commitment to *do* love even when we do not *feel* it.

Taking It Home

Individual Application

- Meditate on Colossians 3:12-14. How would your relationship be different if you were able to live this out more fully?
- A man whose marriage had been unraveling said that things changed dramatically when he took the focus off himself and what

he could do to change his wife and began looking at how he could minister to her. Prayerfully consider how *you* can minister to the man or woman you love, and begin doing some of these things this week.

- Read Matthew 7:1-5. What are the implications for a love relationship found in this passage? Is there a speck in anyone's eye that you have been trying to remove? What are the logs in your own eye?
- Read the First Letter of John (near the end of the New Testament). What in this letter speaks to you? What do you learn about love from this letter?

Couple Application

- Author John Gottman encourages couples to work on developing "love maps" of each other—detailed information about how each person thinks, what each person enjoys, and what is going on in each person's life. Go somewhere you enjoy being together, and begin compiling your own "love maps." Have fun with this!
- Discuss and list ways you can cultivate your friendship. Choose one to begin working on this week.

The Habits of Unhealthy Marriages

Main Idea: Over time, destructive habits can weaken and destroy even the strongest of relationships.

Getting Started

Session Goals
This session is intended to help participants ...
- recognize five habits that cause problems in relationships, often destroying them;
- seek to overcome these destructive habits;
- explore one essential good habit of a successful and lasting relationship.

Opening Prayer
Dear God, we admit that we fall so short of your will for our lives. We make mistakes every day in thought, word, or deed—some small and some big. We ask you to forgive us and make us whole again. Lord, today we ask you to make us right with you and to tear down the walls that threaten to separate us and destroy our relationships. Give us the discernment and wisdom not only to acknowledge our destructive habits but also to overcome them. In Jesus' name we pray. Amen.

Biblical Foundation
So then, putting away falsehood, let all of us speak the truth to our neighbors, for we are members of one another. Be angry but do not sin;

43

do not let the sun go down on your anger, and do not make room for the devil.... Let no evil talk come out of your mouths, but only what is useful for building up, as there is need, so that your words may give grace to those who hear. And do not grieve the Holy Spirit of God, with which you were marked with a seal for the day of redemption. Put away from you all bitterness and wrath and anger and wrangling and slander, together with all malice, and be kind to one another, tenderhearted, forgiving one another, as God in Christ has forgiven you.

(Ephesians 4:25-32)

Opening Activity

Identify some of the common "warning signs" of a marriage that is in danger by playing an old, familiar children's game. Have participants sit in a circle and complete this sentence one at a time: "A marriage is in danger when ..." Each person must repeat what the others have said in order and then add his or her own idea. Write the "warning signs" on the board as participants name them.

Learning Together

Video Presentation

Play the video/DVD segment for Week 5, *The Habits of Unhealthy Marriages.*
Running Time 15:15

Key Insights

Five habits of unhealthy relationships:

1. **Disrespect, contempt, criticism, and abuse.** Neither men nor women can thrive in a relationship in which they are treated in these ways. Abuse literally destroys individuals and families. Sometimes individuals live up to what we say about them. A man or woman who is constantly told that he or she is a failure is likely to live like one eventually. Conversely, men and women who experience five times more praise and encouragement than criticism generally will seek to live up to that praise.

2. **Dishonesty and lying.** Lasting relationships are based upon trust. When a man or woman lies to the other, it undermines the very foundation of their relationship (Proverbs 6:16-19; 10:18; 12:22; Isaiah 59:12-13; Colossians 3:9-10).

3. **Poor handling of money.** Few things have as much power to destroy a healthy relationship as money. This is especially true when we are faced with debt, which often is a result of living beyond our means. (See the biblical principles included in the Leader Extra.)

4. **Alcohol and drug abuse.** These destructive habits generally do not result in the sudden death of a marriage; more often the death is slow and painful. If you do not consider yourself to be an alcohol or drug abuser and yet the person closest to you is being affected negatively, then your habit is interfering with your relationship.

5. **Infidelity.** Having a physically or emotionally intimate relationship outside of marriage is utterly destructive to a marriage. Every portion of Scripture—the Law, the Prophets, the Writings, the Gospels, and the Epistles—condemns extramarital affairs. (Note: We will focus on infidelity in Week 7.)

One essential habit of any healthy relationship:
Forgiveness. No love relationship can survive without the use of six words: "I am sorry," and "I forgive you." Forgiveness is in many ways the central theme of the Christian faith (Matthew 6:14-15; 18:21-22; Mark 11:25; Colossians 2:13-14; 3:13).

Leader Extra
Biblical principles for handling money:
• *Prioritize.* We must seek God first, above all else, and put our complete trust in God—not in material security. We also must be careful about the value we place on money and material things. Money and possessions are not evil in themselves; it is the value we place upon them and the purposes for which we use them that determine whether they are good or evil (Matthew 6:19-21, 24, 25-33; 7:7-11; Luke 12:13-21, 22-31; 1 Timothy 6:10).

- *Tithe regularly, and give generously.* Tithing is the practice of making offerings to God from the first of what we have, not the last. The Bible teaches that we are to give the first tenth of what we earn to God. This principle is meant to provide resources for God's work as well as to bless us and keep our priorities in line. We are to give generously not only to God but also to those in need—especially those in the body of believers (2 Chronicles 31:5; Psalm 37:21; Luke 3:11; Romans 12:13; 2 Corinthians 8:8-15; 9:6-7; Ephesians 4:28; 1 Timothy 6:18).
- *Live within our means.* We are not to use money, expenditures, or possessions as a means of building our self-esteem, impressing others, or trying to fill the emptiness in our lives. That emptiness can be filled only by God (Ecclesiastes 5:10-12; 1 Timothy 6:9-10).
- *Avoid debt.* The Bible says we are to borrow modestly and cautiously, always repaying what we owe to others (Psalm 37:21; Proverbs 3:27-28).
- *Save.* God wants us to be wise stewards by setting aside provisions for future needs—both our own and those of others (Proverbs 6:6-8; 21:20; 2 Corinthians 8:13-15).

Group Discussion

1. How would you define an "unhealthy marriage"? Give some examples.
2. In her book *When Love Dies,* Judy Bodmer tells of a time when she was frustrated with her husband and came to realize that he was like a Van Gogh: If she looked too closely, he was a mess; but if she stood back and saw the "big picture," he was beautiful. Discuss the wisdom of stepping back to look at the man or woman you love and see the "big picture." What can help you to do this?
3. Read Ephesians 4:26. How can you be angry but not sin? Practically speaking, what does it mean not to let the sun go down on your anger? How can you share your feelings honestly yet constructively—without inflicting hurt?
4. Why is trust the foundation of every lasting relationship? What does trust "look like" in a love relationship? Give some examples to illustrate.

5. Do you believe lying is ever permissible or advisable in a love relationship? Why or why not? What about "little white lies"? (See Proverbs 6:16-19; 10:18; 12:22; Isaiah 59:12-13; Colossians 3:9-10.)
6. Discuss some of the common problems couples have that are related to money. What are some biblical principles that can help a couple address these problems? (See the Leader Extra.)
7. What are some of the warning signs of a substance abuse problem? What can you do when the man or woman you love is having difficulty with alcohol or drugs yet refuses to admit it or to address the problem?
8. Why is infidelity utterly destructive to a marriage? (Note: We will discuss infidelity at length in Week 7.)
9. Read Matthew 19:19b and Luke 6:31. How can adhering to these two biblical principles help couples minimize virtually all their destructive habits?
10. How has this discussion helped or challenged you?

Group Activity
Divide participants into groups of three to five. Have them use their Bibles to locate as many scriptural principles for a successful, lasting marriage as they can in the allotted time (other than Matthew 19:19b and Luke 6:31, which were discussed previously). Come back together and have the groups share their lists.

Wrapping Up

Taking It Home
Briefly review the Taking It Home application exercises included in the Participant Handout. Encourage participants to complete the activities during the coming week, reminding them that they will not be asked to share any details with the group. The exercises are intended for their private use and are designed to help them get the most out of this study that they possibly can.

Invite those who have purchased copies of the participant's book to read Chapter 5 this week as a follow-up to this group session.

(Those reading chapters in advance of the group sessions will read Chapter 6 this week.)

Notable Quote
"When you choose to harbor bitterness and resentment, you destroy your own soul; and you miss an opportunity to transform another person by the power of grace."
—Adam Hamilton

Closing Prayer
Lord God, thank you for the truths you have shown us today; and thank you for the unending mercy you continue to shower upon us. Help us to forgive as you have forgiven us. Help us to be grace-filled people who demonstrate the love of Christ. Make us strong and beautiful within, so that our relationships and families will flourish—even during the storms of life. In Jesus' name we pray. Amen.

Week 5: The Habits of Unhealthy Marriages
Participant Handout

So then, putting away falsehood, let all of us speak the truth to our neighbors, for we are members of one another. Be angry but do not sin; do not let the sun go down on your anger, and do not make room for the devil.... Let no evil talk come out of your mouths, but only what is useful for building up, as there is need, so that your words may give grace to those who hear. And do not grieve the Holy Spirit of God, with which you were marked with a seal for the day of redemption. Put away from you all bitterness and wrath and anger and wrangling and slander, together with all malice, and be kind to one another, tenderhearted, forgiving one another, as God in Christ has forgiven you. (Ephesians 4:25-32)

Key Insights

Five destructive habits:
1. Disrespect, contempt, criticism, abuse (Sometimes individuals live up to what we say about them.)
2. Dishonesty and lying (Lasting relationships are based on trust.)
3. Poor handling of money (Check your priorities; tithe; live within your means.)
4. Alcohol and drug abuse (Ask: Is the person closest to me affected negatively?)
5. Infidelity (This can be physical or emotional.)

One essential habit:
Forgiveness (This is in many ways the major theme of our faith.)

Taking It Home

Individual Application
- Read Romans 12:9-10. Imagine a relationship in which both parties outdo each other in showing honor. What might that look like? How might you lead the way?
- Read Ephesians 4:26-27, 29-32. Use these verses as an outline for

prayer. If you have difficulty controlling your anger or are physically or verbally abusive, counseling is an important step in overcoming this habit.

- Read Proverbs 6:16-19, 12:22, and Colossians 3:9-10. How does lying undermine the security of a relationship as well as your integrity and relationship with Christ? In what ways do you or have you struggled with dishonesty?
- Read Proverbs 20:1 and Ephesians 5:18. Are there times when alcohol or drugs are an issue for you? Do loved ones ever express concern in this area?
- The apostle Paul warns, "Don't allow love to turn into lust, setting off a downhill slide into sexual promiscuity" (Ephesians 5:3, *The Message,* NT). What are some of the ways we allow love to turn into lust? How can you guard against this?
- Read Matthew 18:15-35 and Ephesians 4:29-32. What are the implications of these passages for your life?

Couple Application

- All couples disagree about money from time to time. Problems arise when we regularly overspend or misuse money to meet our own needs. Read Malachi 3:8-10, Luke 12:13-34, and 1 Timothy 6:9-10. Discuss ways you can put God first in your money management practices.
- Discuss any of the other habits that are causing problems in your relationship. Consider steps each of you can take to address these concerns.
- Prayerfully consider the ways you need to seek and offer forgiveness to each other, asking the Holy Spirit to enable you to extend and receive forgiveness. Agree to let go of past hurts and allow Christ's love and mercy to bring healing and reconciliation where needed.

God's Plan for Sexual Intimacy

Main Idea: When we understand and follow God's plan for sexual intimacy, the gift becomes a blessing. When we misuse the gift, the consequences can be tragic.

Getting Started

Session Goals
This session is intended to help participants ...
- understand God's plan and purposes for the gift of sexual intimacy;
- view sexual intimacy as a holy act intended for a husband and wife;
- consider the dangers of premarital sex and pornography;
- remember that, through Christ, we can begin again and have a fresh start.

Opening Prayer
Dear God, we come together to discuss a subject that may be sensitive and even painful for some of us; and so we ask you to prepare us as only you can. Open our eyes, our ears, our hearts, and our minds so that we may receive all you have for each one of us here today. Equip us to live the holy lives you have called us to live, through the power of your Holy Spirit. In Jesus' name we pray. Amen.

Biblical Foundation
Therefore a man leaves his father and his mother and clings to his wife, and they become one flesh. And the man and his wife were both naked, and were not ashamed. (Genesis 2:24-25)

For this is the will of God, your sanctification: that you abstain from fornication; that each one of you know how to control your own body in holiness and honor, not with lustful passion, like the Gentiles who do not know God; that no one wrong or exploit a brother or sister in this matter, because the Lord is an avenger in all these things, just as we have already told you beforehand and solemnly warned you. For God did not call us to impurity but in holiness. Therefore whoever rejects this rejects not human authority but God, who also gives his Holy Spirit to you.

(1 Thessalonians 4:3-8)

Opening Activity
Have participants brainstorm a list of words and phrases describing the world's views on sex. What "messages" about sex do we get from the media and popular culture (TV, movies, video and computer games, magazines, music/music videos, the Internet, fashion trends, and so forth)? Write your list on a board or chart.

Learning Together

Video Presentation
Play the video/DVD segment for Week 6, *God's Plan for Sexual Intimacy.*
Running Time 15:09

Key Insights
1. Sex is God's idea. God designed us to be male and female, intended these differences to bring pleasure, and gave us our biological and emotional drives. Sexual intimacy is a thing of beauty meant to produce joy between a husband and wife.
2. God designed sexual intercourse as the method for procreation. It is meant to be a holy act in which we participate with God in creation. It is the means by which life is formed. Too often we forget this powerful purpose of sexual intimacy. A couple must be ready to participate in and accept the responsibility of co-creating with God before beginning a sexual relationship.

3. God designed sexual intercourse as a means of emotional bonding within the covenant of marriage. Genesis 2:24-25 is a euphemistic way of describing sexual intercourse. This physical act corresponds to the emotional and spiritual love spouses have for each other and is meant to bond husband and wife together for a lifetime (See also Mark 10:6-8.).

4. Sex outside of marriage is not in God's plan (Proverbs 5:18-20; 1 Corinthians 7:2; Hebrews 13:4). Here are several reasons:

• Our bodies are God's property and temples of the Holy Spirit; sexual sin defiles God's temple and the union we have with God through the Holy Spirit (1 Corinthians 6:13b, 15-19). We are called to honor God with our bodies, which is an act of spiritual worship (1 Corinthians 6:13b, 15a, 20).

• Premarital sex does not show adequate respect for this holy act associated with the "co-creation" of children.

• Sex unites a man and woman physically, emotionally, and spiritually. Two individuals who have not entered into a covenant relationship yet are joining themselves at the deepest level to each other are perverting God's purpose of bonding through the act of becoming one flesh.

• Virginity is something that can be given away only one time. Premarital sex robs an individual's future spouse of the blessing of being the first one he or she has given himself or herself to.

• There is the possibility of emotional harm and pain—not only to the individuals involved but also to current or future spouses and/or children.

• Sexually transmitted diseases are spread through premarital and extramarital sex, even by people we trust. There are fifteen million new cases of sexually transmitted diseases each year. One in four sexually active teens will contract an STD,[1] which will cost some youth their lives.

• Growing in a sexual relationship is something learned over years in the context of a covenant relationship with one person. It is not learned from repeated attempts to get it right with a variety of people. Such experimentation is a poor way to determine whether to commit to marry another person.

5. Pornography takes what was meant to be good and beautiful and turns it into something cheap and shameful. It places unhealthy and unrealistic images in the mind, promoting lust of the eyes and lust of the flesh—which are never satisfied. (In Matthew 5:28, Jesus equates thinking about sexual sin with the act of committing the sin.) Pornography is addictive, producing a physiological effect that leaves an individual craving more. It enslaves people to their cravings and can open the door to other sins—compulsiveness, selfishness, envy, lying, anger, abuse, violence, and hatred. (See the tips for breaking free of pornography included in the Leader Extra.)

6. God's gift of sexual intimacy is available to us no matter how far we have strayed. Christ provides the love and support we need to bring back the beauty and joy of genuine sexual intimacy.

Leader Extra

Saving Yourself for Marriage
Our biological and emotional drives, coupled with our own fallen nature, make saving ourselves for marriage a challenge. Here are some suggestions:

• Do not put yourself in a situation where you know you will be tempted to compromise. This means not being alone with your date in a place where you may succumb to pressure. (Parents: Know where your kids are. They may not like it, but it is your job to protect them. Find out what time the movie gets out. Know where to reach your kids. Invite them to end the evening at your home. Hold out high expectations—and then offer grace if they fail.)

• Acknowledge that you belong to Christ and your body is the temple of the Holy Spirit; decide in advance that you want to honor God by abstaining from sex until marriage (See 1 Corinthians 6:18-20.).

• Do not set a "limit" that will be difficult to keep in the heat of the moment. Make the boundaries clear to the person you are dating. (Remember that fornication is not limited to sexual intercourse. It includes any form of genital contact.)

Leader Extra

Breaking Free From Pornography

For the Addict

- Seek outside help. Talk with a pastor or trusted Christian counselor.
- Pray, asking God to show you how to break free from your addiction. Remember that it is the Holy Spirit who enables us to "die" to our sinful desires and live for God (Romans 8:1-17).
- Do not allow feelings of shame or guilt to convince you that you are beyond forgiveness. Remember that Christ cleanses us from *all* our sins.
- Draw upon God's strength to fight temptations. You *will fail* if you rely only on your own strength (Romans 8:13). Trust God to increase your self-control (Galatians 5:22-23).
- Change Internet access and e-mail accounts to a filtered Internet provider.
- Install a content filter.
- Move your computer to an open location.
- Purge your computer files of all porn images and programs.
- Erase all porn sites from your "favorites" folder in your Internet browser.
- Delete all "cookie" files.
- Disable cookie file use on your web browser (Banner "teaser" ads may query your cookie files.).
- Run a clean-up program to ensure all the Internet clutter is gone.
- Install a pop-up ad-blocking program.
- Destroy any porn literature you have.
- Destroy magazines and cancel subscriptions (including mailing lists) that are sources of temptation.
- Un-subscribe to cable channels that offer porn or sexually explicit entertainment.
- Destroy any sexually explicit videos.
- Destroy video games that depict sexual acts or contain images that cause you to experience lust.

- Carefully monitor your exposure to radio stations and television programs containing sexual content or sexually stimulating discussions and images.
- Spend time with God each day in a personal "quiet time." Read and learn God's promises (See 2 Corinthians 7:1.).
- Post key Bible verses in visible places (for example, computer monitor, bedroom, bathroom, workshop, office) and review and recite them often.
- Read books and listen to teaching tapes that encourage and strengthen your faith.
- Watch videos and DVD's that edify the family and affirm biblical values.
- Do not lose hope; believe in God for your healing.

For the Spouse
- Do not convict your spouse; pray for the ability to forgive.
- Show your spouse love despite how you feel. Adopt a "tough love" approach, setting clear boundaries for behavior and consequences for crossing them.
- Seek God, draw upon God's strength, and "put on the whole armor of God" (Ephesians 6:11).
- Pray for your spouse.
- Talk with your spouse openly and honestly.
- Do not believe lies such as, "It's your fault" or "There's no hope."
- Do not visit the porn sites your spouse has been visiting.
- Talk to your pastor or a trusted Christian counselor.
- Do not lose hope. Trust God for your spouse's healing.

Group Discussion
1. Read Genesis 1:26-31. What do we learn about God's plan for human sexuality from this passage? Now read Genesis 2:22-25. What can we deduce about God's view of sexuality from this passage? Finally, read Genesis 3:1-7. What impact does human sin have on human sexuality?
2. For what two specific purposes did God create human sexuality? Why are these purposes intended for the covenant of marriage only? (See the information included in Key Insights.)

3. How does premarital sex damage God's gift of sexual intimacy? How would you explain to a young teen why he or she should wait until marriage to experience sexual intimacy? (Again, see the information included in Key Insights.)
4. If sexual intimacy is intended by God to help a man and woman bond emotionally, why do you think sexual relationships between those who are unmarried tend not to last? Why is the commitment of a covenant relationship important to successful bonding? Why is the breakup of a sexually active unmarried couple often just as painful as a divorce?
5. How does adultery damage God's gift of sexual intimacy? (Note: We will explore this topic in detail next week.)
6. Why is pornography a sin? In what ways does it destroy a relationship? What important steps can someone who is struggling with a sexual addiction take? (See the Leader Extra.)
7. How has God provided for those who fall short of God's plan for sexual intimacy? How can we begin again? What role does forgiveness play?
8. How has this discussion helped or challenged you?

Group Activity
At the beginning of the session, you listed the world's views on sex. Now list words and phrases describing God's views on sex. Compare the two lists.

Wrapping Up

Taking It Home
Briefly review the Taking It Home application exercises included in the Participant Handout. Encourage participants to complete the activities during the coming week, reminding them that they will not be asked to share any details with the group. The exercises are intended for their private use and are designed to help them get the most out of this study that they possibly can.

Invite those who have purchased copies of the participant's book to read Chapter 6 this week as a follow-up to this group session.

(Those reading chapters in advance of the group sessions will read Chapter 7 this week.)

Notable Quote

"God's gift of sexual intimacy is available to you no matter how far you have strayed. Don't be confused by what the world says. Trust in Jesus. He will provide the love and support you need to bring back the beauty and joy of genuine sexual intimacy."

—*Adam Hamilton*

Closing Prayer

Lord God, you know all our thoughts and secrets and mistakes; yet you never stop loving us. We turn to you now and ask you to forgive us, heal us, and restore our lives. Help us to follow your beautiful plan for sexual intimacy, so that this gift may be a blessing in our lives. Give us the strength and the courage to be the people you want us to be each and every day. In Jesus' name we pray. Amen.

---

[1] From www.ashastd.org/stdfaqs/statistics.html

Week 6: God's Plan for Sexual Intimacy
Participant Handout

Therefore a man leaves his father and his mother and clings to his wife, and they become one flesh. And the man and his wife were both naked, and were not ashamed. (Genesis 2:24-25)

For this is the will of God, your sanctification: that you abstain from fornication; that each one of you know how to control your own body in holiness and honor, not with lustful passion, like the Gentiles who do not know God; that no one wrong or exploit a brother or sister in this matter, because the Lord is an avenger in all these things, just as we have already told you beforehand and solemnly warned you. For God did not call us to impurity but in holiness. Therefore whoever rejects this rejects not human authority but God, who also gives his Holy Spirit to you.
(1 Thessalonians 4:3-8)

Key Insights
1. Sexual intimacy is a thing of beauty meant to bring joy between a husband and wife.
2. God designed sexual intercourse as the method for procreation. It is a holy act in which we participate with God in creation.
3. God designed sexual intercourse as a means of emotional bonding (Genesis 2:24-25). This physical act corresponds to our emotional and spiritual love for each other and is meant to bond husband and wife together.
4. Sex outside marriage is not in God's plan:
   • Premarital sex defiles God's temple—our bodies (1 Corinthians 6:13b, 15-19).
   • Premarital sex does not show adequate respect for this holy act associated with the "co-creation" of children.
   • We have yet to commit to be one through the bond of marriage, yet we are joining ourselves at the deepest level to another human being. This perverts God's purpose of bonding through becoming one flesh.
   • We can give away our virginity only once.

- There is the possibility of emotional harm and pain. When the relationship ends, in effect, we "divorce" the person with whom we have bonded.
- Sexually transmitted diseases are spread through premarital sex.
- Growing in a sexual relationship is something learned over years in a covenant relationship with one person.
- Relationships involving premarital sex forge bonds before promises have been made.
5. Pornography places unhealthy and unrealistic images in our minds. It takes something beautiful and makes it cheap and shameful. It also is addictive.
6. God's gift of sexual intimacy is available to us no matter how far we have strayed. Christ provides the love and support we need to bring back the beauty and joy of genuine sexual intimacy.

Taking It Home

Individual Application
- Read Leviticus 18; see also Leviticus 20. What timeless principles do you see behind these laws intended for ancient Israel?
- Read 1 Thessalonians 4:1-8. What does this teach us about sex? How does this relate to your life? What is the relationship between our spiritual life and our sex life?
- Read 1 Corinthians 6:12-20. What are the implications of this passage for you? If you are struggling with sexual addiction, talk with a pastor or Christian counselor.
- Read Luke 7:36-50. Describe the heart of Jesus in this passage. What are the implications of this passage for your life?

Couple Application
- Read 1 Corinthians 7:1-7, Galatians 5:22-23, and 1 John 3:16-18. How is sex an opportunity for living the gospel toward each other? Talk and pray with your spouse about how you can better minister to each other in the area of emotional and physical intimacy.

The Ministry and Meaning of Faithfulness

Main Idea: Faithfulness is not simply avoiding an affair; faithfulness has to do with ministering to our mates.

Getting Started

Session Goals

This session is intended to help participants ...

• consider what the Bible has to say about adultery;
• remember that the promise to be faithful is a serious part of the marriage covenant;
• understand the danger of feeding sexual thoughts and fantasies about someone other than a spouse;
• talk with their spouses about how they can help each other remain faithful.

Opening Prayer

Dear God, your steadfast love never ceases. Your mercies never come to an end; they are new every morning. Great is your faithfulness! Forgive us for our *unfaithfulness*. O God, give us undivided hearts so that we may walk in your truth and be faithful—to you and to each other. Amen.

(Prayer based on Lamentations 3:22-23; Psalm 86:11-13)

Biblical Foundation

For everything created by God is good, and nothing is to be rejected, provided it is received with thanksgiving; for it is sanctified by God's word and by prayer. (1 Timothy 4:4-5)

Let marriage be held in honor by all, and let the marriage bed be kept undefiled. (Hebrews 13:4a)

Opening Activity

Have participants name ways that God has been faithful to them. List these on one side of a chart or board. Discuss: How does this list help us to understand what it means to be faithful?

Learning Together

Video Presentation

Play the video/DVD segment for Week 7, *The Ministry and Meaning of Faithfulness.*
Running Time 15:38

Key Insights

1. Sexuality was created by God to be a blessing that bonds a husband and wife together.
2. When we misuse God's gift of sexuality and are unfaithful, it brings negative consequences and extreme pain.
3. Here are some ways to "affair-proof" a marriage:
   - Have a clear conviction that adultery is wrong. (The Bible is clear on this; "Thou shalt not commit adultery" is the seventh commandment.)
   - Do not feed sexual thoughts and fantasies about someone other than your spouse. (When such thoughts come your way, choke them off.)
   - Invite your mate to help you remain faithful. (Do not keep secrets.)
   - Do not spend extended periods of time alone with someone of the opposite sex.

- Do not enter into intimate conversation with someone of the opposite sex. (If you open the door to intimate thoughts and feelings in conversations, you are opening the door to physical behavior.)
- If you have feelings for another person other than your spouse, keep your feelings to yourself because words have power.

4. When it comes to faithfulness in marriage, infidelity is not limited to sexual relations. Jesus defined it as having to do with the thoughts of our hearts (Matthew 5:27-30). Stepping over the line through e-mail, letters, phone calls, or other communication gives a false sense of emotional intimacy or excitement.

5. Sexual intimacy is a gift that gets better over time as husband and wife learn the "dance." It becomes a blessing when they seek to meet each other's needs with no regard for their own needs. This is called agape love.

Leader Extra

The Key to True Intimacy and Faithfulness

The key to building a healthy, intimate relationship is found in the Christian concept of *agape*. This is a kind of love that is primarily focused on meeting the needs of others rather than one's own needs. This love is about serving, blessing, and giving one's self away.

It is in the practice of agape, not in reading about the latest sexual techniques and purchasing the most exotic lingerie, that a satisfying intimate relationship can be built. This can occur when a man and woman each say, "How can I bless my mate, without regard for what I will get in return?" When a husband and wife see sexual intimacy as an opportunity to minister, not as a duty or need, it becomes something wonderful. When romance, affectionate touch, and sexual intimacy are understood as ways of following Christ and living our faith, these practices take on a deeper meaning and become a profound part of our relationship.

It is here that the real meaning of faithfulness comes in. Faithfulness is not simply avoiding an affair. Faithfulness has to do with ministering to our mates, blessing them, and demonstrating a self-giving love that mirrors the love of Christ. This is the basis for discovering the beauty, the blessing, and the bonding that can occur through God's gift of sexual intimacy.

The Bible has numerous passages pertaining to agape love, including 1 Corinthians 13—the familiar "love chapter." See also 1 Corinthians 16:14, Colossians 3:14, 2 Timothy 2:22, and 1 Peter 4:8.

Group Discussion

1. In your own words, explain what it means to be faithful to a spouse. What does it involve? How is being faithful in marriage a "ministry"?
2. Compare how God views adultery to how society and the world view it.
3. What are some of the ways that adultery can begin in a marriage? List some common causes of infidelity.
4. Do you believe adultery is more common today than it was decades ago? Why or why not?
5. List and discuss the ways to affair-proof your marriage as outlined in the video.
6. What are some specific ways spouses can help each other remain faithful?
7. Discuss the dangers of e-mail relationships and other non-sexual activities that can lead to emotional or physical infidelity.
8. Why is sexual intimacy a gift that gets better over time?
9. Give some examples of agape, or sacrificial, love. What happens when this kind of love is practiced within a Christian marriage? (Note: See the Scripture references included in the Leader Extra.)
10. How has this discussion helped or challenged you?

Group Activity

Divide participants into groups of three to five; then have them discuss these questions: What are some of the costs or effects of infidelity, or unfaithfulness, in marriage? What are some of the benefits or effects of fidelity, or faithfulness, in marriage? Come back together and share ideas.

Wrapping Up

Taking It Home

Briefly review the Taking It Home application exercises included in the Participant Handout. Encourage participants to complete the activities during the coming week, reminding them that they will not be asked to share any details with the group. The exercises are intended for their private use and are designed to help them get the most out of this study that they possibly can.

Invite those who have purchased copies of the participant's book to read Chapter 7 this week as a follow-up to this group session. (Those reading chapters in advance of the group sessions will read Chapter 8 this week.)

Notable Quote

"Faithfulness is not simply avoiding an affair. Faithfulness has to do with ministering to our mates, blessing them, and demonstrating a self-giving love that mirrors the love of Christ. This is the basis for discovering the beauty, the blessing, and the bonding that can occur through God's gift of intimacy."

—*Adam Hamilton*

Closing Prayer

Lord God, you know all our hurts and mistakes and fears and hopes and joys. Encourage and strengthen us in our love for you and our love for one another. Bring forgiveness, healing, reconciliation, and wholeness wherever it is needed today. Place a deep desire in each of our hearts to live sacrificially and to minister to our mates' needs. Help us better to understand and experience the pleasure and the blessing of oneness that you intended when you created us male and female. May we grow in faithfulness and love as we make you a partner in our relationships. Amen.

Week 7: The Ministry and Meaning of Faithfulness
Participant Handout

For everything created by God is good, and nothing is to be rejected, provided it is received with thanksgiving; for it is sanctified by God's word and by prayer. (1 Timothy 4:4-5)

Let marriage be held in honor by all, and let the marriage bed be kept undefiled. (Hebrews 13:4a)

Key Insights
1. Sexuality was created by God to be a blessing that bonds a couple together.
2. When we misuse God's gift and are unfaithful, it brings negative consequences and extreme pain.
3. Ways to affair-proof a marriage:
   - Have a clear conviction that adultery is wrong. ("Thou shalt not commit adultery" is the seventh commandment.)
   - Do not feed sexual thoughts and fantasies about someone other than your spouse.
   - Invite your mate to help you remain faithful.
   - Do not spend extended periods of time alone with someone of the opposite sex.
   - Do not enter into intimate conversation with someone of the opposite sex.
   - If you have feelings for another person other than your spouse, keep your feelings to yourself because words have power.
4. Infidelity is not limited to sexual relations. Jesus defined it as having to do with the thoughts of our hearts. Stepping over the line through e-mail, phone calls, or other communication gives a false sense of emotional intimacy or excitement.
5. Sexual intimacy is a gift that gets better over time; it becomes a blessing when husband and wife seek to meet each other's needs with no regard for their own needs. This is called agape love.

Taking It Home

Individual Application
- Read Exodus 20:14. Why do you think avoiding this sin was among the foundational commands God gave to Israel? Now read Proverbs 6:23-35, 1 Corinthians 7:2-5, and Hebrews 13:4. Why is adultery warned against in these passages? What effect does adultery have on all parties involved?
- Read Matthew 5:27-30. What is Jesus' point? Are you ever tempted in this way? What can you do to guard against opening the door to an inappropriate relationship?
- Read John 8:1-11. What do we learn about the heart of Jesus from this passage? God is able to forgive us and restore us. Does this mean that all marriages can survive adultery? Why or why not? How is a marriage able to survive adultery?

Couple Application
- Women need affection, romance, and caring words and touch. Men have a strong need for sexual intimacy. Discuss how you can intentionally meet each other's needs while creating an intimate relationship that regularly involves both. How can you minister to your spouse in the way she or he receives intimacy?
- Discuss specific ways you can help each other to guard against infidelity and remain faithful to each other.
- Share your thoughts with each other regarding John 8:1-11 and the related Individual Application questions. If you are dealing with adultery, talk with a pastor or trusted Christian counselor. (Recommended resource: *Torn Asunder: Recovering From Extra-Marital Affairs,* by Dave Carder, Duncan Jaenicke, and David A. Seamands [Moody Publishers, 1995].)

Making Love Last a Lifetime

Main Idea: A strong relationship with Jesus Christ is the foundation of a lasting marriage.

Getting Started

Session Goals

This session is intended to help participants ...

- affirm the unique blessing and opportunity that Christian singles have;
- discuss the foundation of a lasting marriage;
- understand what it means to make Christ a partner in a marriage;
- explore guidelines for relating to a non-Christian spouse.

Opening Prayer

Dear God, we thank you and praise you that your love for us is unfailing and unending. Teach us how to demonstrate this kind of love—*agape* love—for each other. We pray that, with you as our partner, our love relationships *will* last a lifetime! Open our hearts and minds now to receive your wisdom and power and love. In Jesus' name we pray. Amen.

Biblical Foundation

Two are better than one, because they have a good reward for their toil. For if they fall, one will lift up the other; but woe to one who is alone and falls and does not have another to help. Again, if two lie together, they keep warm; but how can one keep warm alone? And though one might prevail against another, two will withstand one. A threefold cord is not quickly broken. (Ecclesiastes 4:9-12)

Opening Activity

Ask each participant to think of a couple who have been happily married for thirty years or longer. (If they do not know of such a couple personally, have them think of a couple they have read or heard about.) Ask: What do you think is the "secret" of this couple's successful relationship? List the responses on a board or chart. Now, post the "Top 10" list of things that make a marriage successful, which the group created in Week 1 of this study. How do the two lists compare? What changes, if any, would the group make to the "Top 10" list now that they have reached the end of this study?

Learning Together

Video Presentation

Play the video/DVD segment for Week 8, *Making Love Last a Lifetime*.
Running Time 12:43

Key Insights

1. Being a Christian single is both a gift and a blessing. Rather than making the search for a mate the primary focus of their lives, singles should let God know the desire of their hearts and "let it go." They should take advantage of their opportunity to be "radically available" to God. Singles still need companionship, however. Being part of a Christian community is extremely important.

2. Marriage is a calling in which two people enter into a covenant with God to minister to each other. It is not primarily an act of love but an act of discipleship, service, and obedience to God. When seen this way, marriage takes on a new meaning and offers the possibility of real joy and satisfaction.

3. For a marriage to be effective, husband and wife must have a shared sense of meaning. This includes not only shared ideals and goals but also a shared calling to serve God *together*. A married couple can accomplish more as husband and wife in service to Christ than either could accomplish alone.

4. One of the most critical things to look for in a mate—or a date— is the other's faith. A Christian needs a spouse who will share his or her faith, values, and life purpose.

5. If a Christian is married to an unbeliever, the unbelieving mate is sanctified, or "made holy," by the believer (1 Corinthians 7:14). In time, the Holy Spirit shines through the believing spouse to the unbelieving spouse. This requires an extraordinary measure of grace and patience. (See the Leader Extra for some practical guidelines.)

6. When you invite Jesus Christ to be "woven" into your marriage, you will be able to withstand all the forces that may pull against your relationship—no matter how strong these forces may be. These things will help you to make Christ a partner in your marriage:
   - Affirm that Jesus Christ is your Lord and Savior.
   - Continue to build a relationship with Christ—individually and together.
   - Read the Bible together, and apply the wisdom of God's Word to your relationship.
   - Pray together.
   - Worship together.
   - Serve God together.

Leader Extra

If you are married to a non-Christian, here are some guidelines to help you share Christ's light and love with your spouse:
- Focus on making yourself a better person—not on what your mate is lacking.
- Look at your mate through the eyes of Christ.
- Gently and sparingly witness to your faith using words that do not cast judgment but do communicate how important your faith is to you.

- Pray for your mate.
- Demonstrate the love of Christ to your mate in tangible ways.
- Invite your mate to attend church with you periodically, but do not pressure him or her.

Group Discussion

1. How has God's timing sometimes been different from your timing? How does it feel when your timing differs from God's? What can help a single Christian who desires to be married to "wait" on God? In what ways is being single a gift and a blessing?

2. Discuss how marriage is an act of discipleship, faithfulness, and obedience to God. Share an illustration from your own marriage or that of someone you know.

3. Why is it important for a couple to share values and goals? Give an example of a shared goal. Why is it also important for a couple to have a shared *purpose*? What should this purpose be for a Christian couple?

4. We have seen how marriage is a calling for two people to serve each other. How is marriage also a calling to serve others? How have you and your spouse—or a couple you know—served God together?

5. What are some of the challenges of being married to a non-Christian? What "do's and don'ts" would you recommend for Christians whose spouses do not share their faith? (See the Leader Extra for ideas.)

6. As you are comfortable, tell about a turning point in your marriage—or the marriage of someone you know—and how it came about.

7. Why is it important to invite Christ to be a partner in marriage? Practically speaking, what does this mean? How does this strengthen a couple's relationship?

8. How has marriage changed you personally? How has it affected your faith? If single, how has marriage changed someone you know—for better or for worse?

9. If you could give only one sentence of advice to an engaged couple, what would it be? If single, what one question would you like to ask a couple who have been happily married for decades?

10. How has this discussion helped or challenged you?

Group Activity

Give each participant one-to-three index cards, and have the participants write an important or beneficial insight they have gained from this study on each card. Then instruct them to turn their cards over and write an action they will take or a goal they will work toward that is related to each insight. When everyone is finished, invite participants to share at least one insight with the group and, as they are comfortable, one goal or action. (Inform participants that they will need these cards for the Taking It Home exercises this week.)

Wrapping Up

Taking It Home

Briefly review the Taking It Home application exercises included in the Participant Handout. Encourage participants to complete these final activities, which will prepare them for *ongoing* application in the weeks and months to come.

Invite those who have purchased copies of the participant's book to read Chapter 8 this week as a follow-up to this group session.

Notable Quote

"The greatest experiences in your marriage ... are when you ... begin serving other people outside your relationship.... It's the time when you volunteer to teach children in Sunday school or the moments when you serve God together in a host of different ways—when you finally say, "What is God calling us to do together as a team ... so we can serve his kingdom?"

—Adam Hamilton

Closing Prayer

Lord God, thank you for all you have taught us about your purpose and plan for love, marriage, and sex during the course of this study. Forgive us for the ways that we have fallen short of your perfect plan; and help us to forgive each other, just as you have forgiven us. O God, bring healing and wholeness to our hearts and our relationships. Help us fully to surrender ourselves to you each and every day so that we may experience your will for our lives. Help us to remember that love is a choice, not a feeling, and that marriage is a holy and sacred calling to minister to another human being, not a self-centered relationship designed to meet our own needs. Most of all, Lord, help us to make you a partner in our love relationships so that we may draw ever closer to you and to each other. In Jesus' name we pray. Amen.

Week 8: Making Love Last a Lifetime
Participant Handout

Two are better than one, because they have a good reward for their toil. For if they fall, one will lift up the other; but woe to one who is alone and falls and does not have another to help. Again, if two lie together, they keep warm; but how can one keep warm alone? And though one might prevail against another, two will withstand one. A threefold cord is not quickly broken. (Ecclesiastes 4:9-12)

Key Insights

1. Being a Christian single is both a gift and a blessing. It is an opportunity to be "radically available" to God.
2. Marriage is a calling in which two people enter into a covenant with God to minister to each other. It is an act of discipleship, service, and obedience to God.
3. For a marriage to be effective, husband and wife must have a shared sense of purpose or meaning. This includes shared values and goals and a shared calling to serve God *together*.
4. One of the most important things to look for in a mate, or a date, is a shared faith.
5. An unbelieving spouse is sanctified, or "made holy," by a believing spouse (1 Corinthians 7:14). In time, the Holy Spirit shines through the believing spouse to the unbelieving spouse. This requires extraordinary grace and patience.
6. Christ enables you to withstand all the forces that may pull against your relationship. Doing these things will help you to make Christ a partner in your marriage:
   - Affirm Jesus Christ as your Lord and Savior.
   - Continue to build a relationship with Christ—individually and together.
   - Read the Bible together, and apply the wisdom of God's Word to your relationship.
   - Pray together.
   - Worship together.
   - Serve God together.

Taking It Home

Individual Application

- According to Ecclesiastes 4:9-12, why are two better than one? To what does the "threefold cord" refer? How does Christ strengthen a relationship?
- Review your index cards and the goals or actions you listed. Ask God to supply your needs and equip you to follow through.
- Read John 13:1-17. What does Jesus teach us? How is God calling you to serve those closest to you—especially the man or woman you love? Ask God to give you the humble, willing heart of a servant.
- Singles: Read 1 Corinthians 7:14. What are Paul's major points? Verse 17 of 1 Corinthians 7 in *The Message* says, "God, not your marital status, defines your life." What implications does this have for your life?
- Singles: Read 2 Corinthians 6:14. Do you think this passage contradicts 1 Corinthians 7:14 in any way? Why or why not? Why is it advisable not to marry someone who does not share your faith in Christ?

Couple Application

- Discuss your index cards. Ask, "What can I do to encourage you?" Commit to pray for and encourage each other in these areas.
- Share your reflections on John 13:1-17—and, as you are led, the ways God is calling you to serve each other. Take turns washing each other's feet. Let this be a reverent, sacred act expressing your desire to serve God by serving each other. End with a word of prayer together.